50
WOODEN
CRAFTS TO MAKE
WITH KIDS

QUICK AND EASY PROJECTS PARENTS
AND CHILDREN CAN MAK

BY ELLEN J. HOBART AND E'
ILLUSTRATIONS BY PAM

PRINCE PAPERBACKS, NEW YORK

To Michael, Joe and Matt, with all our love

Copyright © 1994 by Ellen J. Hobart and Eva Shaw
Illustrations copyright © 1994 by Pam Posey

Published by Crown Publishers, Inc., 201 East 50th Street, New York, New York 10022. Member of the Crown Publishing Group.

Random House, Inc. New York, Toronto, London, Sydney, Auckland

Prince Paperbacks and colophon are trademarks of Crown Publishers, Inc. Manufactured in the United States of America

Designed by Mercedes Everett

Library of Congress Cataloging-in-Publication Data
Hobart, Ellen J.
Fifty wooden crafts to make with kids / by Ellen J. Hobart and Eva Shaw; illustrations by Pam Posey.
p. cm.
1. Woodwork. I. Shaw, Eva 1947–. II. Posey, Pam.
III. Title.
TT185. H657 1994
684'.08—dc20
93-21213
CIP
ISBN 0-517-88175-6

10 9 8 7 6 5 4 3 2 1

First Edition

Acknowledgments

We want to thank our families and friends for receiving (graciously and enthusiastically!) our handmade crafts throughout the years.

Special thanks to Mom and Daddy-O (Janet and Dave), Lars and Vick, Chris and Laurie, Kurt, Nancy and Tim, Mil and Ed, Debby and Phil, Ginger, and the rest of our clans. And in loving memory of Ellen's Seedy and Eva's Uncle John.

Linear and Area Measures

1 inch	2.54 centimeters
1 foot	0.3048 meters
1 square inch	6.4516 square centimeters
1 square foot	929.03 square centimeters

CONTENTS

INTRODUCTION

SECTION I:
TOYS AND GAMES

SECTION II:
FUN CRAFTS FOR THE GARDEN

SECTION III:
HOME DECORATIONS

SECTION IV:
HOLIDAY DECORATIONS..............65

SECTION V:
GIFTS 81

INTRODUCTION

Making crafts is fun. It's a rewarding activity for children, parents, caregivers, scout leaders, and teachers. The crafts described in this book are for children from five to twelve as well as their older helpers. Everyone can have a positive experience as well as a lasting one.

Creating and building these crafts can be a family event that will produce games and gifts for friends, teachers, grandparents, and other special folks. There are decorations for inside as well as outside and plenty of activities for the December holidays.

Projects are suitable for family craft-making days, rainy days, fun days, and camp and scouting activities. The end results are quality projects of which children can be proud.

Sure, craft-making takes time, but it's also an excellent example of recycling materials to produce a toy, game, gift, or garden decoration. All you need is a little planning, patience, and love, and the crafts will be successful every time.

A NOTE TO PARENTS, TEACHERS, CAREGIVERS, AND ESPECIALLY FOR CHILDREN

All the crafts are suitable for children to make, but, the child's involvement in the activity will depend on adult participation. The crafts provide the caregiver with wonderful opportunities to teach the safe use of tools, to spend time with a child, and to create something special by hand.

It is recommended before starting the crafts that you and the child do the practice sessions to learn the correct use of tools and equipment. You should both read the instructions, assemble all the materials, and plan how you will work together. This is especially important if more than one child is working on the craft or many children are working at the same time.

Every craft requires some use of a saw to cut the wood. For the youngest ones, an adult will have to do all the cutting. If you do not know how to operate a saw or other tools, ask a friend for help. Before you purchase any supplies, check to determine if you can recycle materials from home improvement projects, pieces of wood from neighbors or lumberyards, paint and sandpaper from other crafts. Sometimes the wood is already in the right shape for the craft. All the measurements given are approximate, so you can easily adapt the projects to suit materials you have. Where the pieces of wood seem especially long, it's often possible to use several pieces that equal the total amount required.

Let's say you want to make the cat scratching post, and in the garage there's a piece of wood that's 4 inches square but a few inches longer or shorter than the directions indicate. You can use this piece; there's no need to cut it before nailing it to the wooden base. Just modify the instructions accordingly.

Even the youngest child can help select the right size piece of scrap wood, talk about the directions, and plan how the project will be built. It's exciting and educational for small children to know the names of tools, and the specific uses for each, and to participate in the sanding, painting, and decorating of the projects. You'll not only be making crafts that are fun, but you'll be making memories, too.

The skill level is based on the difficulty of the craft after the wood has been cut. For example, the Tugboat is recommended for a child six to nine years of age) because hammering is involved. Yet, a five- or six-year-old could easily do the sanding and painting as well as tie the string for the boat's guardrail.

This is true for all the crafts in the book. Every child can be involved in some level of assembly. Since you know the child's skill level best, look at all the projects, regardless of skill level, but check the Skill Level Key that follows. Additionally, if you use these crafts as a project to teach and stimulate a child's thinking, you can even get a three- or four-year-old involved.

All crafts require wood that must be cut with a saw and sanded. Many crafts can be painted, and if painting is recommended, it is indicated. All crafts that require hammering, gluing, or the use of a screwdriver, drill, or jigsaw are also noted.

Use your creativity: Items you already have around the house or workshop can be used to change the projects or to decorate them in different ways. For example, instead of using a button to trim the top of the bookmark, a small shell would be pretty. On the garden bench, why not paint flowers, birds, or the child's name? The tin can pencil holder can be decorated by gluing uncooked pasta, beans, or buttons to the covering. Make the crafts your very own by personalizing them for yourself or the person who will receive them. Have fun!

SKILL LEVEL KEY

 = **5- TO 6-YEAR-OLD CHILD**. After a practice session and reviewing instructions, and with adult supervision, the child can sand, paint, and use a marking pen and glue (wood and white glue).

 = **6- TO 9-YEAR-OLD CHILD.** After a practice session and reviewing instructions, and with adult supervision, the child can sand, paint, glue (wood and white), and use a ruler, marking pen, screwdriver, and hammer.

 = **9- TO 12-YEAR-OLD CHILD**. After a practice session and reviewing instructions, and with adult supervision, the child can sand, paint, glue (wood and white), and use a marking pen, ruler, screwdriver, hammer, saw, and drill.

LET'S PRACTICE SAFETY

A pencil is a tool. You use it to draw lines. Hammers and nails are also tools, but they don't come with erasers. When using woodworking tools, the best way to avoid getting hurt or making a mistake on the craft is by being careful. Being careful takes practice.

These are some of the tools you will be using to make the crafts and projects in this book.

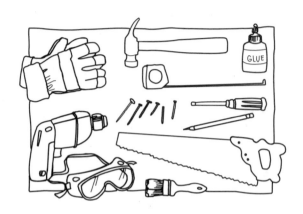

PRACTICE USING SANDPAPER

Using a scrap of sandpaper, look at the edges of a piece of wood. Are they rough? Sand the edge of a piece of wood until it feels smooth to your fingers. Practice sanding the flat sides of the wood. Always sand in the direction of the grain.

You may want to make a sanding block by wrapping sandpaper around a small piece of wood that fits into your hand well. The rough side of the sandpaper goes on the outside. Sanding blocks are used to smooth large flat wooden surfaces. All the projects in this book will need to be sanded.

PRACTICE USING A HAMMER AND NAILS

Hammer five nails into a large scrap of wood, until the heads are flat against the wood. Then hammer in five other nails until the head of each nail is halfway into the wood. Use the claw end of the hammer to take out some of the nails.

PRACTICE USING A SCREWDRIVER

Using a flathead screwdriver and flathead wood screws, twist the screws into a scrap of wood. Sometimes when a piece of wood is very hard, it is easier to hammer a nail into the wood first to make a small hole. The nail is then taken out and the screw can be twisted into the wood more easily.

PRACTICE USING GLUE

Wood glue is used to stick pieces of wood together; you can also use white glue, but wood glue sticks better to pieces of wood. Glue is messy, but it will come off your hands with soap and water.

Practice using wood glue. Find one large piece and four small pieces of scrap wood. Squeeze wood glue onto one side of each small piece, using slightly more glue for each but not so much that the glue drips over the edges. Place the pieces on the large piece of wood.

Allow the glue to dry according to the directions on the container. Now decide how much glue is necessary to make the pieces stick. The right amount of glue will not show on the sides, nor will it allow the piece to wiggle.

PRACTICE USING A SAW

Using a pencil and a ruler, mark a piece of scrap wood with lines you can saw. Do not mark them too close together because this will making sawing difficult. Hold a saw in one hand and the long side of the wood in the other hand. Carefully cut through the wood.

PRACTICE USING A DRILL

Put a large piece of scrap wood underneath the practice piece before drilling holes to protect the surface on which you're working in case the drill goes too deep.

Using a pencil, mark a number of small x's on a large piece of scrap wood. Make sure a drill bit is in the drill. Hold a power drill directly above the center of the mark so that the drill is perpendicular to the wood. Lower the drill to the mark and carefully apply pressure to the power switch. Drill the hole, remove the drill from the hole, and release the power switch. Always make sure that a power tool is completely off before putting it down.

Drill some holes completely through the wood and others halfway.

PRACTICE USING PAINT AND A BRUSH

Using scrap wood, water-based paint, and a small brush (about 1 inch wide), paint the wood. Remember that all paint needs to dry before you can continue with the craft and before you can paint another color next to or over the first color.

Always apply the paint with the grain. Be sure to wash and dry the brush so that you can use it again.

PRACTICE USING SCISSORS

Hold paper in one hand and cut various shapes using a pair of scissors. You also may want to practice cutting yarn or rope.

GENERAL INSTRUCTIONS AND SUGGESTIONS

1. Tools are not toys. Be sure to talk about their safe use before you begin. Always put tools, nails, and other craftmaking material away when you finish the crafts. While making the crafts in this book, you can teach safe ways to use tools.

2. All crafts require the cutting of wood, so it is understood that you will need a saw. Other needed items are listed in the directions.

3. Sometimes you can use scraps of wood that do not need to be cut. This makes the craft slightly different, so you may have to change other parts, which is some of the fun.

4. When hammering and sawing, be sure to wear protective goggles. You may want to wear gloves when sanding, gluing, and painting.

5. When using a power tool, always turn off the tool before putting it down. Always pull out the plug when not in use. Never use a tool near water, and never permit a child to use one without adult supervision.

6. Use only water-based, nontoxic paint for the projects unless otherwise noted. These are called acrylic paints. When painting, make sure that clothing and work surfaces are covered to protect them from spills. Always let the paint dry before going on to the next step of the craft. Wash hands and brushes well when finished for the day.

7. Sometimes it's best to make a paper pattern for the craft before you begin. Cut out the pattern and use a pencil to lightly trace around it onto your piece of wood. Then cut out the shape you traced. This works especially well if you're making many of the same craft.

8. Use marking pens that are nontoxic and washable. Sometimes the ink from marking pens must dry before you can touch it. Test your pens on some scrap wood before you use them on your craft. Be sure to cover the pens when they're not in use.

9. Use a fine grade of sandpaper. The higher the number printed on the back of the sandpaper, the smoother the sanding will be. We recommend #280 grade.

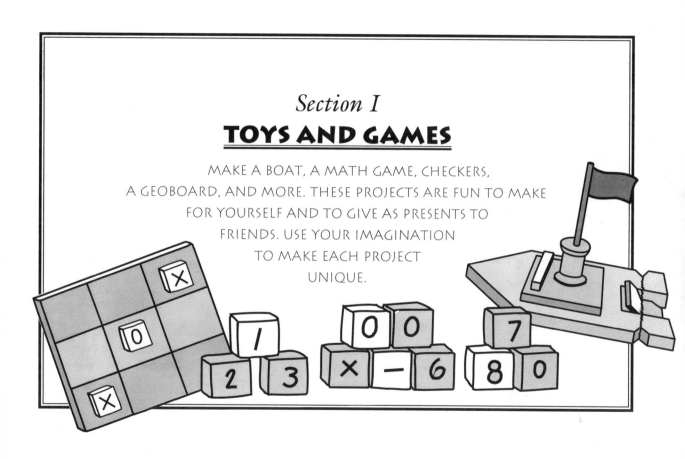

Section I
TOYS AND GAMES

MAKE A BOAT, A MATH GAME, CHECKERS,
A GEOBOARD, AND MORE. THESE PROJECTS ARE FUN TO MAKE
FOR YOURSELF AND TO GIVE AS PRESENTS TO
FRIENDS. USE YOUR IMAGINATION
TO MAKE EACH PROJECT
UNIQUE.

TUGBOAT

LEVEL 2 — If you live near a pond, have a kiddie pool, or want to motor around the carpet pretending your tugboat is in open water, this craft will be fun for you.

WHAT YOU'LL NEED

WOOD: 1 piece not more than ½ inch thick, 6 to 8 inches long, and 4 inches wide; 1 square piece 2 inches on each side; 1 smaller square about 1 inch on each side

SANDPAPER

NAILS: 4 long nails that will connect the blocks to the rectangle; 44 small nails

STRING OR YARN

PAINT AND A PAINTBRUSH

WHAT TO DO

1. The piece of wood you choose is the boat, and the top is called the deck. If you want, cut the bow (or front) of the tugboat into a point, or you can leave it square.

2. Nail the 2-inch-square piece of wood to the boat and nail the 1-inch-square piece on top of the 2-inch piece. This is the cabin.

3. Sand all the edges.

4. Hammer small nails only halfway into the wood every ½ inch around the edges of the deck.

5. Paint.

6. Starting at the front of the boat, loop a piece of string around each of the small nails. This forms the guardrail around the deck.

SAILBOAT

LEVEL 3

A real sailboat can be bigger than a car and longer than a house. People sail across the ocean. This toy sailboat can be fun in the tub or even in a puddle.

WHAT YOU'LL NEED

WOOD: 1 piece not more than ½ inch thick, 6 to 8 inches long, and 4 inches wide

SANDPAPER

STIFF PAPER, such as construction paper

1/2-INCH DOWEL, the same length as the boat

GLUE

A DRILL

WHAT TO DO

1. Cut the base (hull) of the boat, making a point on one end. This will be the front, or bow, of the boat.

2. Drill a hole the same circumference as the dowel, stopping before you drill through to the other side, about ⅛ of the way from the front or the pointed end of the boat.

3. Sand all the edges.

4. Cut the dowel about the same length as the boat.

5. Cut the paper about 2 inches shorter than the dowel. The width should be slightly smaller than the length. This will be the sail.

6. Cut two slits in the "sail," about ½ inch from each end.

7. Put the dowel through one slit and out the other.

8. Glue the dowel into the drilled hole in the boat.

PADDLEBOAT

Would you like to make boats and race them with friends or with your mom or dad? This paddleboat takes a little time to make, but you'll have hours of fun with it when it's finished.

WHAT YOU'LL NEED

WOOD: 1 piece no thicker than ½ inch, 6 inches wide, and 8 inches long; 1 piece 1½-inches long and 2 inches wide of a flat and thin variety (such as balsa); various shapes and sizes of wood scraps

SANDPAPER

1/2-INCH-DIAMETER DOWEL OR SPOOL; a 2-inch dowel looks good

A RUBBER BAND a little smaller than the width of the wood

A TOOTHPICK OR SMALL DRINKING STRAW

A PIECE OF PAPER OR FABRIC for a flag

WHAT TO DO

1. Cut the ½-inch-thick wood the size you want your boat, making a point on one end. This will be the front of the boat (see directions for Sailboat).

2. Cut a notch in the back of the boat, about 2 inches by 2 inches.

3. Cut two very small notches in the outside edges, one on each side, about 1 inch from the back or flat end of the boat. These notches should only be big enough for the rubber band to slip into.

4. Cut the propeller out of the balsalike wood, about 1½ inches by 1¾ inches.

5. Cut two very small notches in the propeller. These notches should be located in the middle of the 1½-inch sides.

6. Sand the edges of the boat and the propeller.

7. Glue small pieces of wood, the dowel and/or the spool, on top of the boat (see illustration). Be careful you don't make it too heavy!

8. Wrap the rubber band around the propeller, making sure it's in the notches. Slip the propeller in the 2-inch notch in the back of the boat. Secure it in place by slipping the rubber band in the outside small notches of the boat.

The twisted rubber band will unwind, propelling the paddle, and the boat, through the water.

STILTS

Stilts take practice to use, and you must have good balance and coordination. Be sure to have someone hold you when you're just learning to walk with them. When you are able to use them well, you might enjoy having relay races on stilts.

WHAT YOU'LL NEED

WOOD: 2 pieces 2 inches square and about 1 or 2 feet longer than the height of the person who will use the stilts; 1 piece 2 inches thick, 4 inches wide (called a two-by-four), and 20 inches long for footrests

SANDPAPER

4 SCREWS 1 INCH LONG

2 SHORTER SCREWS

GLUE

WHAT TO DO

1. From the two-by-four cut two 10-inch-long pieces in the shape of right triangles. These will be the footrests. The top side of the footrests (or base of the triangle) should be slightly wider than the feet of the person using the stilts.

2. Sand all the edges.

3. Glue one side of the footrest against the two-by-two so that the top of the footrest is 6 inches to 12 inches from the bottom of the stilt (the height depends on the height of the person using the stilts).

4. When the glue dries, screw two of the 2-inch screws through the stilts into each footrest near its top. Screw one of the smaller screws through the stilt into the bottom of each footrest.

BUILDING BLOCKS

LEVEL 1 You can build space stations, castles, towns, and cities with these blocks. You can drive toy cars through the streets, hide action figures behind the buildings, or land rockets on top of the towers.

WHAT YOU'LL NEED

WOOD: various shapes and sizes, widths and lengths

SANDPAPER

PAINT AND A PAINTBRUSH

WHAT TO DO

1. Cut the wood into various shapes. Cut some with pointed tops and some with flat tops. Cut some in small pieces and others in large shapes, or you can find scraps of wood that are already cut. You want blocks of various sizes—chunky, little, long, and short.

2. Sand all the edges until they are smooth to the touch.

3. Paint the blocks in various colors. Let the blocks dry.

4. You can paint doors and windows on some of the blocks. You can paint trees or flowers on them, too.

ALPHABET BLOCKS

 Learn the alphabet, spell words, or create a spelling game with these alphabet blocks.

WHAT YOU'LL NEED

WOOD: 1 or more pieces 1 inch thick and 3 inches wide, or 2-inch-square pieces that equal 104 inches or longer, or other sizes that can be cut into block shapes. Remember, you want to make at least 26 finished blocks.

SANDPAPER

PAINT OR A MARKING PEN for drawing the letters. You may want to buy stencils of letters of the alphabet, or you can paint or draw the letters on the blocks yourself.

WHAT TO DO

1. Cut pieces of wood into 2-inch pieces.

2. Sand all the edges.

3. Draw, paint, or stencil the letters of the alphabet on the blocks. Let the blocks dry.

4. If you're going to make a spelling game, you may want to make up extra blocks so that you have plenty of letters. For example, make three blocks with the letter *A*, three blocks with the letter *E*, and all of the other vowel letters. It's always handy to have extra blocks with *N*, *P*, *S*, and *T*, too.

NUMBER BLOCKS AND MATH BLOCKS

Learn your numbers or improve your math skills with these blocks. If you're already good at adding and subtracting, make blocks showing the signs for multiplication and division. You can make up fraction and percentage blocks, too.

WHAT YOU'LL NEED

WOOD: 1 or more pieces 1 inch thick and 3 inches wide, or 2-inch-square pieces that equal 104 inches or longer, or other sizes that can be cut into block shapes.

SANDPAPER

PAINT, MARKING PEN, AND/OR STENCILS for marking the numbers on wooden blocks

WHAT TO DO

1. Cut pieces of wood into 2-inch pieces.

2. Sand all the edges.

3. Draw, paint, or stencil the numbers from 0 to 9 on the wooden blocks. You can also make blocks showing the math signs: ×, −, +, ÷, =. Remember, if you paint the blocks first, you should let them dry before putting on the numbers.

4. If you're going to play a math game, you may want to make up extra blocks so that you have plenty of numbers.

TIC-TAC-TOE GAME

Everybody loves to play tic-tac-toe. Make your own game that you can use over and over.

WHAT YOU'LL NEED

WOOD: 1 piece that measures 12 inches square and 6 blocks of wood that measure 1 inch square

SANDPAPER

A RULER

PAINT AND A BRUSH, OR A MARKING PEN

WHAT TO DO

1. Sand the edges of the large square. This is your tic-tac-toe board.

2. Using a ruler and a pencil, measure and mark the board like a tic-tac-toe game, with lines every 4 inches. Each square should measure 4 inches square.

3. With paint or a marking pen, place the game lines on the board. Allow it to dry.

4. While the board is drying, sand all the edges of the game pieces. Paint three blocks one color and three another color. Be sure to let the game pieces dry before placing the X or O on them using paint or a marking pen. Wait again for the second color to dry before playing.

CHECKERS

An old-time favorite for everyone in the family, this is a great game to take in the car, on a picnic, or when visiting friends.

WHAT YOU'LL NEED

WOOD: 1 piece that measures 18 inches square and at least ½ inch thick

SANDPAPER

RED AND BLACK PAINT

2-INCH DOWEL AT LEAST 12 INCHES LONG

A RULER

BLACK FELT TIP PEN (optional)

WHAT TO DO

1. If not already done, cut the wood into an 18-inch square. This will be the playing board.

2. Sand all the edges.

3. With a ruler, mark a 1-inch border all around the playing board. Divide the rest of the playing board (inside the border) into sixty-four 2-inch squares (eight squares by eight squares), using a pencil to outline the squares. Go over the pencil marks with a felt tip pen or with black paint, using a small, fine, paintbrush and a steady hand!

4. Paint alternating squares black and red.

5. Cut the dowel into twenty-four pieces, about 1/2 inch thick.

6. Sand all the edges.

7. Paint twelve of the pieces red and twelve of the pieces black.

PADDLEBALL RACKETS

LEVEL 2

Fun for children, teens, and parents! Use Ping-Pong balls for the paddleball and make up games as you go along.

WHAT YOU'LL NEED

WOOD: ¼-inch-thick or ⅜-inch-thick plywood at least 8 inches wide and 30 inches long. This is enough for 2 paddles.

SANDPAPER

A JIGSAW

FOAM RUBBER

GLUE

BLACK ELECTRICAL TAPE (optional)

WHAT TO DO

1. Trace the shape of a paddle on the plywood. The handle should be about 5 inches long, the paddle about 10 inches long by 7½ inches wide.

2. Cut out the paddle with a jigsaw.

3. Sand all the edges.

4. Cut two pieces the size of the handle out of the scrap and glue them to either side of the handle to build it up. Wrap black electrical tape around the handle for a better grip.

5. For smaller children, cut two pieces of foam rubber the same size as the handle and glue them to either side.

BALANCE BOARD

It's fun to see who can balance the longest on this balance board. Playing with the balance board will help you to learn the balancing skills you need when playing sports and riding bikes.

WHAT YOU'LL NEED

WOOD: 1 piece of exterior plywood or something similar at least 16 inches by 16 inches and ¾ inch thick; one 4-inch-square piece.

SANDPAPER

4 FLATHEAD WOOD SCREWS, 1 1/2 INCHES LONG

4 STRIPS OF SANDPAPER, 1/2 INCH BY 14 INCHES

A DRILL

A SCREWDRIVER

GLUE

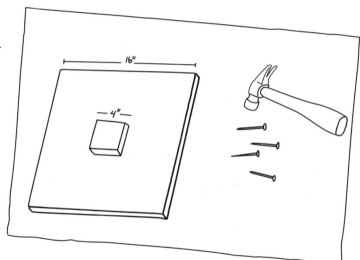

WHAT TO DO

1. Cut the plywood into a 16-inch square if it's not already this size. This is the balance board.

2. Mark a 3-inch square in the center of the board and drill four holes just inside the corners of the square for the wood screws.

3. Cut the 3-inch by 3-inch block for the base if it has not already been done.

4. Sand all the edges.

5. Screw the 3-inch by 3-inch block into the bottom with the wood screws.

6. Glue sandpaper strips on top of the board so that feet won't slip.

RING AND TOSS TARGET

LEVEL 2

Everybody likes to play games. The ring and toss target game takes practice, and the better you get, the more fun you can have.

WHAT YOU'LL NEED

WOOD: 1 piece 1 inch thick, 4 inches wide, and about 18 to 20 inches long

1/2 INCH DOWEL 18 INCHES LONG OR 3 PEGS 6 INCHES LONG

SANDPAPER

PAINT (you choose the color)

GLUE

A DRILL

WHAT TO DO

1. Sand the edges of the 1-inch by 4-inch board.

2. Drill three holes no wider than the dowels, one on either end and one in the middle.

3. Cut the dowel into three pieces, each about 6 inches long.

4. Glue the dowels into the three holes.

5. Paint

GEOBOARD

LEVEL 2

With this handy board you can make shapes, designs, and even pictures. A geoboard is reusable, too, because when you've finished one design, you can remove the rubber bands and make another.

WHAT YOU'LL NEED

WOOD: 1 piece 6 inches square and at least ½ inch thick
SANDPAPER
25 NAILS 1 1/2 INCHES LONG
RUBBER BANDS (different colored ones are best)
PAINT (optional)

WHAT TO DO

1. Sand all the edges.

2. Paint the board if desired. Black is a good color since it shows the different-colored rubber bands.

3. Allowing a 1-inch border all around, mark the board for placement of the nails 1 inch apart; mark five rows of five nails in each row.

4. At the marks hammer the nails in far enough so they are secure (without going all the way through the board). Do not hammer them in so far that the rubber bands cannot be looped around them.

5. Loop the rubber bands around the nails to make different shapes and designs.

HOBBY HORSE

Make your own hobby horse and gallop around your backyard, ride at the park, or trot inside your house on rainy days. Don't forget to give your horse a special name.

WHAT YOU'LL NEED

WOOD: 1 piece 4 inches square and 8 inches long. This is the head.

1 LARGE DOWEL AT LEAST 3/4 INCH IN DIAMETER OR AN OLD BROOM HANDLE
The dowel should be cut so that it is slightly higher than the child's waist. This is the body.

SANDPAPER

A DRILL WITH A DRILL BIT TO CUT A 3/4- INCH HOLE IN THE 4-INCH-SQUARE PIECE OF WOOD

WOOD GLUE

PAINT

STRING, YARN, ROPE, OR FABRIC FOR MANE AND REINS

2 NAILS 1 INCH LONG to attach the reins

WHAT TO DO

1. Drill a hole approximately 2 inches deep into the wood for the head, about 1 inch from the end of the board. Sand the horse's head and around the edges of the hole.

2. Hammer a nail in each side of the head, in about the middle. Let the nail stick out about ¼ inch.

3. Place wood glue in the hole for the dowel and place the dowel in the hole. Allow to dry.

4. After the glue is dry, tie a 3-foot piece of rope, string, or yarn to each nail. These are the reins.

5. Using white glue, put pieces of rope, yarn, string, or fabric along the top of the horse's head. You can even make a bow and put it in your horse's mane.

6. Paint eyes and a happy smile on your horse.

7. Allow the paint to dry before galloping around.

Section II
FUN CRAFTS FOR THE GARDEN

THE CRAFTS AND PROJECTS IN THIS SECTION
ARE MEANT TO BE USED OUTDOORS. IF YOU PAINT THE
WOOD OR PUT A WATER SEALER ON IT, THE PROJECTS
WILL LAST AND LOOK NICER
FOR A LONGER TIME.

BIRD FEEDER

Would you like to feed the birds that visit your backyard? Here is an easy-to-build feeder you can make right now.

WHAT YOU'LL NEED

WOOD: 1 piece 12 inches square and ½ inch thick (plywood works well); 4 pieces of molding or thin strips 12 inches long and about ½ inch square. For the post, one piece 4 inches square and 5 or 6 feet long.

SANDPAPER

GLUE

4 LARGE NAILS to secure the feeder to the post

EXTERIOR HOUSE PAINT

WHAT TO DO

1. Sand all the edges.

2. Using wood glue, attach the thin strips of wood or molding to one side of the 12-inch square. These are the sides that keep the birdseed from falling to the ground. If you want, you can

TRAY TOP VIEW

4"x4" POST

use small nails instead of glue. This is the seed tray.

3. To place the tray in the center of the post, locate the middle of the 12-inch seed tray and mark this place with a pencil.

4. Attach the post to the seed tray using at least four nails.

5. Paint the seed tray and post.

6. Dig a hole in your garden, place the bird feeder into the hole, and pack the dirt around the post. You can place rocks or bricks on the ground close to the post to make it more secure.

7. Put birdseed in the tray. You can put peanuts, sunflower seeds, tiny bits of bread, or slices of fruit in the tray for the birds, too.

8. You can keep a journal of all the types of birds you see. The public library has books about birds so you can learn their names, what they like to eat, and where they live.

(NOTE: So that the birds feel safe, place the bird feeder away from trees and buildings.)

STAKES FOR FLOWER, VEGETABLE, AND HERB GARDENS

LEVEL 1

These flower, vegetable, and herb garden signs make pots on the windowsill look cute. In the garden they look pretty and identify what has been planted in the rows. They're fun to make and to give as presents to people who like to work in the garden.

WHAT YOU'LL NEED

WOOD: Several pieces 1 inch thick and 3 inches wide. You will need 1 piece of wood for every stake you plan to make.

SANDPAPER

PAINT

WHAT TO DO

1. Cut the strips of wood into 12-inch pieces. If you're using tongue depressors, you do not need to cut them.

2. Sand all the edges.

3. Paint the stakes. Allow the paint to dry.

4. Write the names of the flowers, vegetables, or herbs that the stakes will be used for. You can also paint flowers and vegetables on the stakes.

5. Push the stakes into the ground next to the plants you want to identify.

VARIATION: If you're making plant stakes for small indoor plants and herbs, you can use craft sticks, which look like tongue depressors. You can buy them at the hobby or craft store. Be sure to decorate them and write the name of the plant or herb for which the stake will be used.

WINDOW BOX OR PLANTER

LEVEL 3

Make this window box or planter in one afternoon. All you need to have a beautiful garden are potting soil, seeds, and water. Garden stores have lots of plants and seeds. You can also buy seeds at the supermarket. Follow the instructions when you grow plants, and your window box or planter will be pretty.

WHAT YOU'LL NEED

WOOD: 1 piece about 1 inch thick, 12 inches wide, and 96 inches (8 feet) long (redwood is recommended)

SANDPAPER

ABOUT 40 NAILS 1 INCH LONG

A DRILL

OUTDOOR PAINT OR FINISH (optional)

WHAT TO DO

1. Cut three pieces of wood 24 inches long (these are the bottom and two sides). Cut two pieces 10 inches long (these are the ends). Cut two pieces 2 inches long (these will be the "feet").

2. Drill four holes in what will be the bottom of the planter for drainage.

3. Sand all the edges.

4. Place one of the 24-inch pieces on the bottom of the planter and nail in place. This makes half of the side of the planter. Repeat with the other 24-inch side piece.

5. Insert the 10-inch end pieces into the ends of the planter and nail in place.

6. Turn the planter over and nail the "feet" onto the bottom, placing them near either end and making sure you don't cover any drainage holes.

7. If using redwood, the planter does not need to be sealed or painted. If another type of wood is used, seal or paint the entire planter inside and out with a water sealer or outdoor paint.

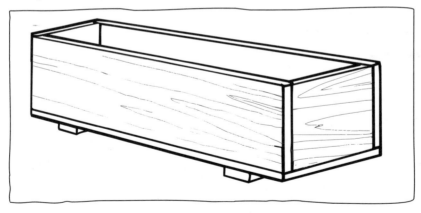

GARDEN BENCH

LEVEL 2

Every garden needs a bench. This one is a favorite for children and adults who like to be outdoors and work in the yard.

WHAT YOU'LL NEED

WOOD: 1 piece about 1½ inches thick, 12 inches wide, and 80 inches long; 1 piece that is 1½ inches thick, 3½ inches wide, and 33 inches long

SANDPAPER
24 NAILS 1 INCH LONG
OUTDOOR PAINT OR FINISH

WHAT TO DO

1. Out of the 12-inch-wide wood cut a piece that is 48 inches long. This will be the seat.

2. Out of the remainder of the 12-inch wood, cut two pieces that are 16 inches long each. These will be the two legs.

3. Sand all the edges.

4. Place the end of one leg about 6 inches in from the end of the seat. Nail in place.

5. Do the same with the other leg, placing it about 6 inches in from the other end of the seat. Nail in place.

6. Out of the 3½ inch-wide-wood cut a piece that will fit between the two legs. Sand all the edges.

7. Place this piece about halfway down, between the legs, and nail in place. This acts as a brace and lends more support to the bench.

8. Paint with outdoor paint or finish with a water sealer.

Section III

HOME DECORATIONS

THE CRAFTS IN THIS SECTION ARE EASY
TO MAKE AND USEFUL, TOO. THERE ARE BOOKENDS,
A PAPER TOWEL HOLDER, AND A RACK TO HANG YOUR JACKET,
JUMP ROPE, AND MITTENS. REMEMBER, ALL MEASUREMENTS ARE
APPROXIMATE TO ALLOW YOU TO USE
WHATEVER WOOD IS HANDY.

HOUSE-SHAPED NAPKIN HOLDER

This paper napkin holder in the shape of a house can also be used as a letter holder.

WHAT YOU'LL NEED

WOOD: 1 piece about ⅛ inch thick, 12 inches wide, and 6 inches long, cut into two 6-inch squares, and 1 piece about 1 inch thick, 3 inches wide, and 6 inches long

A RULER

SANDPAPER

8 SMALL NAILS (ask for "finishing" nails)

PAINT

WHAT TO DO

1. Once the thin wood is cut into two 6-inch squares, find the center of one side on each square. Mark this center with a pencil. This is the peak of the house's roof. On the sides, measure down 2 inches from the top corner. Using a ruler, draw a straight line from the center mark to the mark on the side. Mark and make cutting lines on both pieces of wood.

2. Cut along these lines.

3. Sand all the pieces of wood.

4. Attach the 1-inch-thick by 3-inch-wide piece of wood to the bottom of the house sides, using small finishing nails.

5. Paint the house and allow to dry. Then, using another color, paint a door, windows, flowers, and trees. Let the paint dry before using the finished project.

BOOKENDS

LEVEL 2 Reading is even more fun when you have a place to keep your books. This is a good item to make as a gift for friends and your family, too.

WHAT YOU'LL NEED

WOOD: 2 pieces about 1 inch thick, 5 inches wide, and 9 inches long

SANDPAPER

6 NAILS 1 INCH LONG

PAINT

WHAT TO DO

1. Cut two pieces of wood about 5 inches square for the backs and two pieces of wood about 5 inches by 4 inches for the bases.

2. Sand all the edges

3. Using nails, attach the back to the base so an "L" shape is formed.

4. Paint and decorate with scrap wood or personalize by painting initials or names on them. Or use other materials such as shells, stickers, or cutout designs to customize your bookends.

DOORSTOP

 Doorstops are attractive, and they're handy to keep the door open on a breezy day.

WHAT YOU'LL NEED

WOOD: 1 piece about ½ inch thick, 5 inches wide, and 9 inches long

SANDPAPER

3 NAILS 1 INCH LONG

PAINT

WHAT TO DO

1. Cut a piece of wood about 5 inches square for the doorstop and a piece of wood about 5 inches by 4 inches for the base.

2. Sand all the edges.

3. Using nails, attach the back to the base so an "L" shape is formed.

4. Paint and decorate the doorstop.

"SEEDY" STOOL

LEVEL 3 **T**his stool's name is from my grandfather "Seedy." He made a stool just like this for me and all his other grandchildren when we were toddlers. But this stool isn't just for little kids, it's for kids of all sizes. You can sit on it when you're playing a board game or stand on it when you're getting something off a shelf.

WHAT YOU'LL NEED

WOOD: 1 piece about 1 inch thick, 12 inches wide, and 4 feet long

ABOUT 50 NAILS 1 INCH LONG

A JIGSAW

PAINT

WHAT TO DO

1. Cut three pieces of wood 11 inches by 11 inches each (these will be the top or back and two sides). Cut one piece of wood 10½ inches by 11 inches (this will be the seat).

2. Using a jigsaw, cut two holes (handles) at opposite ends of each of the two sides (four handles altogether).

3. Sand all the edges.

4. Nail the two sides to the top or back.

5. Insert the seat between the sides and nail in place.

6. Paint and decorate.

TRAY

LEVEL 2

Do you like to eat a sandwich while sitting on the floor? When you set the table, would you like to carry all the knives, forks, and spoons at one time? Then this tray can help you.

WHAT YOU'LL NEED

WOOD: 1 piece about 12 inches square and ½ inch thick (plywood works well); 4 pieces of wood molding or thin strips 12 inches long and about ½ inch square

SANDPAPER
GLUE
PAINT

WHAT TO DO

1. Sand all the edges.

2. Using wood glue, put the thin strips of wood along the edges of one side of the 12-inch square.

3. Paint the tray.

CUTTING BOARD

LEVEL 1

You can make a cutting board in the shape of a square, a rectangle, or a circle. You can make a cutting board in the shape of a pig or a fish. Be sure to scrub the finished cutting board with dish soap and warm water and let it dry before you use it.

WHAT YOU'LL NEED

WOOD: 1 piece at least 1 inch thick and wide enough to cut fruit or vegetables (see step 1 below)

SANDPAPER

A DRILL (for making a hanging hole, if desired)

WHAT TO DO

1. Saw the board into a shape you want. Cutting boards that are 4 inches wide by 6 inches long are good for making sandwiches. Cutting boards that are 12 inches square are good for chopping vegetables and making salads. Cutting boards that are 2 feet square are good for kneading bread and rolling cookie or pie dough.

2. If you plan to hang the cutting board, drill a hole through the wood about 1 inch from any edge.

3. Sand all the edges and surfaces until the board is very smooth.

4. Wash the cutting board very well with dish soap and warm water before using it and after each use.

CLOTHES AND SPORTS EQUIPMENT RACK

LEVEL 3

Hang this rack so that you can reach it with jackets, sweaters, jump ropes, and anything in your room that needs to be organized.

WHAT YOU'LL NEED

WOOD: 1 piece about 30 inches long by 8 inches wide. Plywood is good for this project. You can make the rack larger or smaller depending on where you plan to put it.

5 PEGS OR A 25-INCH PIECE OF DOWEL CUT INTO 5-INCH PIECES

SANDPAPER

A DRILL

5 WOOD SCREWS that will go through the board and at least 1 inch into the pegs

PAINT
2 PICTURE FRAME HANGERS
WHAT TO DO

1. Sand all the edges.

2. Using a ruler, measure the board and plan where you will drill holes for the pegs. They should be evenly spaced and have room on each side. If your board is 30 inches long, make the first pencil mark 2 inches from one end and then make pencil marks every 6½ inches across the board, leaving 2 inches on the other end.

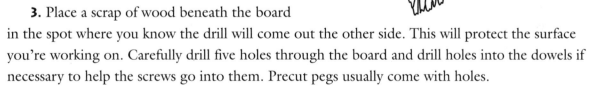

3. Place a scrap of wood beneath the board in the spot where you know the drill will come out the other side. This will protect the surface you're working on. Carefully drill five holes through the board and drill holes into the dowels if necessary to help the screws go into them. Precut pegs usually come with holes.

4. Sand any rough edges.

5. Using a screwdriver and screws, attach the pegs to the board.

6. Paint the board and the pegs and allow to dry.

7. Attach the picture frame hangers to the back of the board.

MUG RACK

LEVEL 3

Hot chocolate mugs, soup mugs, coffee mugs, they all fit and look pretty on this mug rack for the kitchen. What a perfect gift for Mom, Grandma, or Big Brother's first apartment.

WHAT YOU'LL NEED

WOOD: 1 piece about 20 inches long and 5 inches wide (plywood works well). You can make the rack larger or smaller depending on where you plan to put it or how many cups you'd like to hang on it.

5 PEGS OR A 20-INCH PIECE OF DOWEL CUT INTO 4-INCH PIECES

SANDPAPER

A DRILL

5 WOOD SCREWS that will go through the board and at least 1 inch into the pegs. Most pre-cut pegs already come with holes in the base to allow the screws to enter them easily.

PAINT

2 PICTURE FRAME HANGERS

WHAT TO DO

1. Sand all the edges.

2. Using a ruler, measure the board and plan where you will drill holes for the pegs. They should be evenly spaced with room left on each side. If your board is 20 inches long, make the first pencil mark 1 inch from one end and then make pencil marks every 4½ inches across the board, leaving 1 inch on the other end.

3. Place a scrap of wood beneath the board where you know the drill will come out the other side. Carefully drill five holes through the board and drill holes into the dowels if necessary.

4. Sand any rough edges.

5. Using a screwdriver and screws, attach the pegs to the board.

6. Paint the board and allow it to dry.

7. Attach the picture frame hangers to the back of the board.

TRIVET

 This is one of the easiest projects to make and a great gift for anyone on your list.

WHAT YOU'LL NEED

WOOD: 1 piece at least 6 inches square and at least ½ inch thick

SMALL WOODEN PEGS, ROUND WOODEN BALLS, OR SMALL PIECES CUT FROM A DOWEL (4 for each trivet; these are the "feet")

SANDPAPER

GLUE

PAINT

POLYURETHANE (heat resistant)

WHAT TO DO

1. Cut the wood to the desired size. Squares work best, but you can also make your trivet in the shape of a triangle, circle, or other shape. Place the "feet" accordingly.

2. Sand all the edges.

3. Glue one small peg in each corner of the underside of the wood. These are the "feet."

4. Paint as desired.

5. When the paint dries, apply two or three coats of polyurethane, sanding lightly between coats.

PAPER TOWEL HOLDER

LEVEL 2 **W**hy not make a paper towel holder for the garage, the workshop, and the kitchen, too?

WHAT YOU'LL NEED

WOOD: 1 piece 1 inch thick and 6 inches square for the base, which can also be round or triangular

1 DOWEL ABOUT 12 INCHES LONG AND 1 INCH IN DIAMETER; it must be long enough to fit through the roll of paper towels

SANDPAPER

A DRILL

1 WOOD SCREW AT LEAST 2 INCHES LONG

PAINT

WHAT TO DO

1. Sand all the edges.

2. Find the center of the base and drill a small hole through it. Drill a hole a short distance into the dowel.

3. Attach the base to the dowel using the wood screw. The screw should go into the dowel at least 1½ inches.

4. Paint the dowel and allow it to dry.

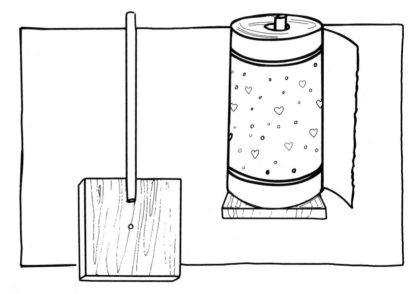

HOUSE KEY HOLDER

LEVEL 3

Here's a "mini" rack for keys. Hang it near the door. Place keys on it as soon as you come home, and you'll always know where your keys are.

WHAT YOU'LL NEED

WOOD: 1 piece cut in the shape of a house, a heart, or a shape of your choice; 1 piece 6 inches square and 1 inch thick works well for this. (You may want to make a paper pattern first to trace onto the wood. This works well if you're making many key holders and want them all the same.)

3 PEGS OR A PIECE OF DOWEL 9 INCHES LONG CUT INTO 3 PIECES

SANDPAPER

A DRILL

3 WOOD SCREWS 3/4 INCH LONG

PAINT

1 PICTURE FRAME HANGER

WHAT TO DO

1. Cut the square of wood into the shape you've chosen.

2. Sand all the edges.

3. Using a pencil and a ruler, mark where you will be placing the pegs.

4. Drill holes through the base at the pencil marks. Drill holes into the dowels. Precut pegs usually come with holes.

5. Attach the pegs to the base using wood screws.

6. Paint and allow to dry. If you're making a heart, you can paint tiny flowers on the key holder. If you're making a house, you can paint windows and a door. Otherwise, you can decorate your base for the room where it will hang.

7. Attach the picture frame hanger to the back of the base.

VARIATION: Use cup-holder-size hooks that screw into wood instead of pegs for hanging the keys.

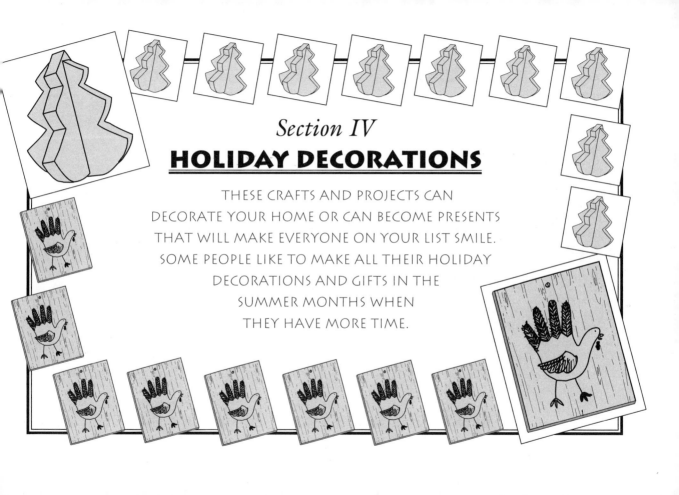

Section IV
HOLIDAY DECORATIONS

THESE CRAFTS AND PROJECTS CAN
DECORATE YOUR HOME OR CAN BECOME PRESENTS
THAT WILL MAKE EVERYONE ON YOUR LIST SMILE.
SOME PEOPLE LIKE TO MAKE ALL THEIR HOLIDAY
DECORATIONS AND GIFTS IN THE
SUMMER MONTHS WHEN
THEY HAVE MORE TIME.

THANKSGIVING TURKEY HAND

LEVEL 1 **E**verybody loves turkey. This turkey is made of wood, so don't try to eat it on Thanksgiving. You can use it to decorate a door or give it to someone special.

WHAT YOU'LL NEED

WOOD: 1 piece about ¼ inch thick and at least 1 inch wider and longer than the hand that will be making the outline for the turkey

SANDPAPER

PENCIL

PAINT

RIBBON, STRING, YARN, OR THIN ROPE

A DRILL

WHAT TO DO

1. Place your hand in the middle of the wood, with fingers spread apart, and trace it.

2. If necessary, cut the wood so that it extends only about 1 inch beyond the traced hand.

3. Drill a hole in the top center of the wood—not within the hand but in the border.

4. Sand all the edges.

5. Add "turkey legs" and "beak" and paint the fingers to look like turkey feathers.

6. Thread ribbon, yarn, string, or other material through the hole at the top and hang it on the wall, around a doorknob, or on a drawer handle.

VARIATION: You can nail a piece of wood behind the base of the turkey to make it a table decoration.

"NOEL" HOUSES

"**N**oel" is another word for Christmas. These Christmas houses can be made any time of the year and put away until December.

WHAT YOU'LL NEED

WOOD: 4 blocks in various sizes, at least 2 inches square and at least 4 inches high

DOWELS 1/4 INCH THICK AND 8 INCHES LONG

SANDPAPER

PAINT

GLUE

A DRILL

WHAT TO DO

1. If not already done, cut four blocks of wood in various heights. Cut the wood to a point on one end, to make it look like the roof of a house.

2. Sand all the edges.

3. Paint all the blocks white.

4. Drill a ¼-inch-wide hole in one side of the "roof" of each block. This is for the chimney.

5. Cut the dowel into four pieces, one for each chimney hole.

6. Sand the dowel edges.

7. Glue one end of the dowel into the holes.

8. Paint the letter *N* on the side of one block, the letter *O* on the side of another, the letter *E* on the side of another, and the letter *L* on the side of the last block. Make them large enough to be seen from across the room.

9. Decorate the other sides of the houses with windows, doors, window boxes, and flowers.

Decorate around the letters, too. Paint the roof black and the chimneys red. You can also glue artificial flowers in the flower boxes or add other details.

CHRISTMAS TREE ORNAMENTS

LEVEL 2 **Y**ou can paint these wooden Christmas tree ornaments in silver, gold, green, or red. Or you can spray them with clear varnish to show off the color of the natural wood. You can also use them to decorate the top of a special gift.

Sometimes you can buy wooden ornaments at the craft store. If you've purchased the ornaments, go right to step 4 below.

WHAT YOU'LL NEED

WOOD: 1 piece about ⅛ inch thick; the size will depend on how many ornaments you plan to make

SANDPAPER

A DRILL

PAPER OR CARDBOARD to make a pattern

PAINT

RIBBON OR YARN

WHAT TO DO

1. Make a pattern for the ornaments using paper or cardboard. You can make ornaments in the shapes of pine trees, hearts, houses, circles, or squares.

2. Cut the thin wood into the shapes you desire.

3. Drill holes in the top of the ornaments about ¼ inch from the edge.

4. Sand all the edges, including around the holes.

5. Paint the ornaments and allow them to dry. You can decorate them by gluing tiny buttons, shells, glitter or paper stars onto the wood. Triangles can be decorated to look like Christmas trees; squares can look like wrapped gift boxes; and on the circles you can glue a picture of a family member.

6. Thread a piece of ribbon or yarn through the hole and make a circle with the yarn about the right size to hang the decoration on the tree.

CHRISTMAS OR HANUKKAH BLOCKS

Every grandparent, teacher, friend, and neighbor will want a set of these blocks that spell **MERRY CHRISTMAS.** You can also make letter blocks to spell **HAPPY EASTER, HAPPY BIRTHDAY, HAPPY HANUKKAH**, or **HAPPY NEW YEAR.** The choice is up to you.

WHAT YOU'LL NEED

WOOD: One or more pieces 1 inch thick and 3 inches wide or 2 inches square that equal 48 inches or longer, or other-sized wood that can be cut into block shapes

SANDPAPER

PAINT OR A MARKING PEN for drawing the letters. You may want to buy stencils with the letters of the alphabet, or you can paint or draw the letters on the blocks yourself.

WHAT TO DO

1. Cut pieces of wood into 2-inch pieces.

2. Sand all the edges.

3. Paint the blocks. Some people like to paint all the blocks white and then use red and green to paint or stencil the letters onto the blocks. Some people like to paint the blocks red and green and then use the opposite color to paint or stencil the letter. If you are making Hanukkah blocks, use silver and blue or gold, and then black, red, or brown for the letters.

4. Draw, paint, or stencil the letters **MERRY CHRISTMAS** onto the blocks. Allow the blocks to dry. Then stack the blocks with **CHRISTMAS** beneath the word **MERRY.** Use the same procedure for **HAPPY HANUKKAH**.

HOLIDAY DOOR TOPPER

LEVEL 2 **W**hether you hang the door topper over the front door or place it on the mantel, everyone will admire it. Take your time with this craft because the little details make it even prettier.

WHAT YOU'LL NEED

WOOD: 1 piece about 1 inch thick, 6 inches wide, and 25 inches long, or other wood approximately this size. Draw a paper or cardboard pattern if you will be making more than 1 door topper and you want them to be uniform.

SANDPAPER

PAINT

2 PICTURE FRAME HANGERS for each door topper

TINY ORNAMENTS such as trees, wreaths, birds, and hearts that are glued onto the door topper village scene (optional)

WHAT TO DO

1. Looking at the illustration opposite, copy the same types of houses onto your pattern or the piece of wood. Use a pencil and ruler to lightly draw all the lines so you can cover them with paint.

2. Cut out the roof shapes.

3. Sand all the edges.

4. Paint all the houses. Let the paint dry, and then paint all the roofs.

5. Paint on the details such as the doors, windows, flowers, and trees. Don't forget to put a big Christmas tree, with painted lights and colorful ornaments, in the middle of the door topper! Allow the paint to dry.

6. Attach the picture frame hangers to the back of the door topper. The picture frame hangers will make the door topper more secure.

3-D CHRISTMAS TREES

LEVEL 1 **S**ome people make a whole "forest" of trees. Start with one. Once you see how easy and fun they are to make, you'll want more—to keep and to give as presents.

WHAT YOU'LL NEED

WOOD: 1 piece about 1 inch thick, 6 inches wide, and 16 inches long, or 2 pieces 8 inches square

SANDPAPER

GREEN PAINT

A BAND SAW

WHAT TO DO

1. Draw the outline of each section of the tree on the wood—about 8 inches high and the full 6 inches wide at the widest.

2. Cut with the band saw.

3. Sand all the edges.

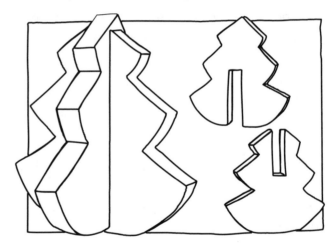

4. Before painting, slip the two pieces together to make sure they fit easily. If not, sand or cut the notches a little more, depending on how much has to be taken off.

5. Paint green.

3-D CHRISTMAS STARS

Make one star or make lots of stars. These stars shine and sparkle if you decorate them with glitter.

WHAT YOU'LL NEED

WOOD: 1 piece about 1 inch thick, 6 inches wide, and at least 14 to 16 inches long for each star, or 2 pieces 7 to 8 inches square

SANDPAPER

SILVER OR GOLD PAINT, or other colors you prefer

GLUE

GLITTER (We like silver and gold, but green looks good, too.)

WHAT TO DO

1. Draw the two outlines of a star on the wood. Like the Christmas tree, draw a line to notch down the top of one star and between the bottom points of the other.

2. Cut with a band saw.

3. Before sanding, slip the two pieces together to make sure they slide in and out easily. If not, sand or cut a little more out of each notch.

4. Sand all the edges.

5. Paint the star.

6. Dab glue on the star or use spray adhesive and sprinkle with glitter. Make a wish!

MENORAH

LEVEL 2 **T**his will be a very special menorah because you've made it. Do you think your grandparents or someone you love would also like one? Then you'd better make at least two!

WHAT YOU'LL NEED

WOOD: 1 piece about ½ inch thick, 2 inches wide, and 19 inches long

1 DOWEL 1 INCH IN DIAMETER AND 17 INCHES LONG (see below)

SANDPAPER

GLUE

9 NAILS 1/2 INCH LONG

A DRILL

9 CANDLES 1/2 INCH WIDE

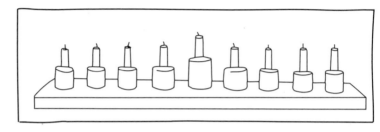

WHAT TO DO

1. Sand all the edges of the wood. This is the base.

2. Cut nine sections out of the dowel as follows (these are the candle holders) or use leftover pieces of dowel to make:

•two **1-INCH PIECES**•two **1 1/2- INCH PIECES**•two **2-INCH PIECES**
•two **2 1/2-INCH PIECES**•one **3-INCH PIECE**

3. Sand the edges of the cut candle holders.

4. Position the candle holders on the base as shown in the illustration. Allow about 1 inch between each holder.

5. Glue in place.

6. Drill a ½-inch-wide hole about halfway down each candle holder.

7. After the glue dries, turn the menorah over and nail each candle holder in place. Be sure to include a box of candles when giving this as a gift!

LOVE BLOCK FOR VALENTINE'S DAY

LEVEL 1 **D**o you know someone special who would love an extra-thoughtful Valentine's gift? These blocks are easy to make, and you'll want to make lots of them so you can give one to Mom, Dad, your aunt, grandparents, and other favorite people.

WHAT YOU'LL NEED
WOOD: 1 piece about 2 inches square for every Love Block you want to make

SANDPAPER

RED PAINT

BLACK AND RED MARKING PENS

WHAT TO DO

1. Sand all the edges.

2. Stencil or paint a red heart on one side of the block.

3. Write to and from on the back of the block with a black marking pen.

4. With the red marking pen, write the name of the person to whom you're giving the block. Next to the word *from* write your own name.

FLAG

Display this project all year instead of just on the Fourth of July. You can make it into a school project by making flags of different countries or by making a copy of the first American flag ever made.

Do you know how many stars and stripes there were on the first flag? You will find information about flags in an encyclopedia.

WHAT YOU'LL NEED

WOOD: 1 piece ¼ inch thick, 9 inches wide, and 12 inches long
SANDPAPER

RED, WHITE, AND BLUE PAINT

ROPE, TWINE, OR YARN

A DRILL

WHAT TO DO

1. Sand all edges.

2. Draw the outline of the flag on the rectangle.

3. Paint the stripes red and white, the stars white, and the background of the star field blue.

4. Drill two holes all the way through the flag, one in each top corner.

5. Loop rope, twine, or heavy yarn through the holes and hang the flag on the wall.

GINNY

Section V
<u>GIFTS</u>

DO YOU KNOW ANY TEACHERS, PARENTS, OR
FRIENDS WHO WOULD LIKE A SPECIAL, MADE-WITH-YOUR-OWN-
HANDS PRESENT? ALL THE CRAFTS IN THIS BOOK CAN BE GIVEN AS
GIFTS. AND IN THIS SECTION YOU'LL DISCOVER CRAFTS AND
PROJECTS THAT ARE TO BE MADE MAINLY AS PRESENTS.
NOW WHAT WILL YOU MAKE FIRST?

FIDO

How Big Am I?
EVA

4

3

2

1

ABC APPLE BLOCKS

 These ABCs are great for your schoolteacher, music teacher, or karate instructor.

WHAT YOU'LL NEED

WOOD: 1 piece about 2 inches thick, 2 inches wide, and 8 inches long; each block requires 2 inches of wood

SANDPAPER

PAINT

STENCILS, PAINT, OR A MARKING PEN for making the letters

WHAT TO DO

1. Cut pieces of wood into 2-inch pieces.

2. Sand all the edges.

3. Paint the blocks. Some people like to paint all the blocks one color, such as white, and then use another bright color for the ABC letters. Other people like to use red paint for *A*, yellow for *B*, blue for *C*, and then white paint for the block on which the red apple is painted.

4. Draw, paint, or stencil *A*, *B*, and *C* on three blocks. On the fourth block draw or paint a bright red apple.

NAME BLOCKS
AND SPECIAL NAME BLOCKS

Will you create blocks that say **SUPER MOM**, **GREATEST DAD**, or **I LOVE GRANDMOTHER**? Here's a chance to make extraordinary name blocks for everybody.

WHAT YOU'LL NEED

WOOD: 1 piece 2 inches thick, 2 inches wide, and 2 inches long for every letter block you want to make. Count your letters first!

SANDPAPER

PAINT

STENCILS, PAINT, OR A MARKING PEN for making the letters

WHAT TO DO

1. Cut pieces of wood into 2-inch pieces.

2. Sand all the edges.

3. Paint the blocks. Some people like to paint the blocks one color, such as red or blue, and then use another bright color for the name that will be spelled with the letters.

4. Draw, paint, or stencil the name on the blocks.

BOOKMARKS

 Everybody needs a bookmark. These are quick and easy to make, and they look great.

WHAT YOU'LL NEED

CRAFT STICKS (they look like long, fat, flat popsicle sticks); tongue depressors work, too

SANDPAPER

PAINT

GLUE

DECORATIONS: buttons, bows, shells, a seedpod

MARKING PEN (if you want to write on the bookmark)

WHAT TO DO

1. Paint the stick on both sides and allow to dry.

2. Glue a decoration on one end. You can decorate both sides of the one end which will stick out of the book.

3. If you want, you can also write something on the bookmark such as **MOM'S BOOK**.

HOW BIG AM I?

LEVEL 2 You can make this project for your own room or for a friend, brother, or sister. Be sure to decorate it—and sign your name if you want.

WHAT YOU'LL NEED

WOOD: 1 piece about ¼ inch thick, 14 inches wide, and 48 inches long

SANDPAPER

1 YARDSTICK

PAINT

GLUE

WHAT TO DO

1. Sand all the edges.

2. Paint all the wood (optional).

3. Glue the yardstick in the center of the wood but closer to one side. This will allow you to write along the side of the yardstick, on the wood, the date when the measurement was taken and who was measured.

4. Decorate the wood around the yardstick with painted flowers, animals, names, or other items.

5. When hanging it on the wall, make sure you measure from the floor so that the height is correct.

ROOM AND SPECIAL NAME SIGNS

LEVEL 2 **W**ould you like to have a sign with your own name on it? This project tells you how to do it. You can make signs for special people, too.

WHAT YOU'LL NEED

WOOD: 1 piece of wood about ¼ inch thick, 4 inches wide, and 12 inches long

SANDPAPER

PAINT

TWINE, STRING, OR YARN

A DRILL

LETTER STENCILS (optional)

WHAT TO DO

1. Cut the wood into a rectangle as long as needed to fit the name or special words that will be printed on it.

2. Sand all the edges.

3. Paint the wood any color.

4. Paint your name or special words in the middle of the wood (use stencils if you want) and decorate with painted flowers, animals, special pictures, or anything you like.

5. Ideas for special words: **SUPER DAD, FAVORITE TEACHER, GREATEST MOM, BEST GRANDMA**

6. Drill two holes in each upper corner of the sign.

7. Loop the twine, string, or yarn through the holes and hang the sign on a door or wall. Or you can glue a piece of wood on the back to make it stand.

CANDLE HOLDERS

Lots of people like to burn candles, and these pretty candle holders are easy to make and fun to give. *Never use matches or light candles without the approval and supervision of an adult!*

WHAT YOU'LL NEED

WOOD: for each candle holder, a block of wood 2 inches thick, 2 inches wide, and 2 inches long, or dowels that are 2 inches in diameter. Scraps of ¼-inch wood for decorations.

SANDPAPER

A DRILL

PAINT

GLUE

CANDLES

WHAT TO DO

1. Sand all the edges of the blocks and/or dowels.

2. Drill holes about 1 inch down and about 1 inch wide in each block.

3. Paint any color.

4. Cut various shapes out of the ¼-inch wood: hearts, Christmas trees, or anything you like. Or buy precut wooden ornaments. Decorate all your favorite way.

5. Sand all the edges.

6. Glue decorations on one side or two opposite sides of the holder.

DOG HOUSE SIGN

LEVEL 2 **S**haped like a bone, this house sign is especially designed for your dog (or a dog you know and like).

WHAT YOU'LL NEED

WOOD: 1 piece large enough to cut a bone shape on which all the letters of the dog's name will fit

SANDPAPER

A DRILL

1 NAIL

PAINT

MARKING PEN OR STENCILS

WHAT TO DO

1. Make a paper pattern of a dog bone the size you'd like to have on your dog's house. Trace the pattern on the wood.

2. Cut the dog bone shape.

3. Sand all the edges.

4. Paint the dog bone a bright color that your dog will like. Allow the paint to dry.

5. Paint, draw, or stencil your dog's name onto the sign.

CAT SCRATCHING POST

LEVEL
3

Don't forget that the pets in your family like to receive gifts. Your feline friend will love this one, especially if you rub catnip on the carpet that you glue to the post!

WHAT YOU'LL NEED

WOOD: 1 piece 1 inch thick, 6 inches wide, and 16 inches long

A DRILL

SANDPAPER

SCRAP CARPETING—short shag or indoor/outdoor works best

WHITE GLUE

24 CARPET TACKS 1/2 INCH LONG

ANY KIND OF ROPE OR HEAVY TWINE

WHAT TO DO

1. If the wood is not already 16 inches long, cut it to size.

2. Drill two holes in one end of the wood, one in each corner.

3. Sand all the edges.

4. Cut the carpet slightly smaller than the wood.

5. Glue the carpet to the wood. Hammer carpet tacks through the carpet in various places to help secure it to the wood.

6. Loop the small rope through the holes, tie the ends together, and hang the post on a doorknob.

NECKLACE

LEVEL 3

Teachers, moms, aunts, and grandmothers will love this necklace that you can make and give as a present. Why not make one for yourself, too?

WHAT YOU'LL NEED

THIN WOOD OR PRECUT WOOD SHAPES such as hearts, circles, squares, or animals that you can buy at the crafts store

SANDPAPER

A DRILL

PAINT

YARN, RIBBON, OR ROPE, long enough to fit over your head when tied and knotted; 3 feet is a good length to start

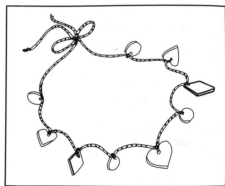

WHAT TO DO

1. If you're cutting the shapes from thin wood, you may want to use a paper pattern so that the sizes are the same. You can cut circles, hearts, houses, and animals. If you're using precut shapes, go right to the next step.

2. Sand all the edges.

3. Drill small holes in the top of each shape.

4. Paint the shapes.

5. String the wood shapes together with yarn, ribbon, or rope, making a knot at the top of each shape so that it stays in one place.

WELCOME FRIENDS BLOCKS

Everybody likes friends. These blocks are extra nice for people who enjoy a warm, country look in their house or apartment.

WHAT YOU'LL NEED

WOOD: 1 piece 2 inches wide, 2 inches thick, and 28 inches long, or more if you're making more than 1 set of blocks!

SANDPAPER

PAINT

STENCILS, PAINT, OR A MARKING PEN for making the letters

WHAT TO DO

1. Cut the wood into 2-inch pieces.

2. Sand all the edges.

3. Paint the blocks and allow the paint to dry before going to step 4. Blue paint looks especially nice on these blocks.

4. Paint or stencil the words **WELCOME FRIENDS** on the blocks. Allow the paint to dry.

TIN CAN PENCIL HOLDER

LEVEL 1

Where does your mom, dad, aunt, uncle, or teacher keep pencils and pens? This project is fun, and the pencil holder looks great on a desk or telephone table. It's easy, and you may want to make them for all your friends and family.

WHAT YOU'LL NEED

1 CLEAN TIN CAN about 4 inches high and with the label removed

ENOUGH TONGUE DEPRESSORS OR POPSICLE STICKS to go around the outside of the can you've chosen

GLUE

PAINT

FELT OR SCRAP MATERIAL (optional)

WHAT TO DO

1. Make sure the tin can is completely clean, inside and out, and that it is free of sharp, rough edges. Get an adult to help.

2. Glue the tongue depressors or popsicle sticks on the outside of the can, covering the entire can so there isn't any metal showing. Depending on the size of the can, you may have to overlap the final tongue depressor.

3. Paint and decorate the tongue depressors or popsicle sticks.

4. If you want, line the inside of the can with felt or some type of material. Line the bottom, too.